Helping Our Planet

Waste and Recycling

Sally Morgan

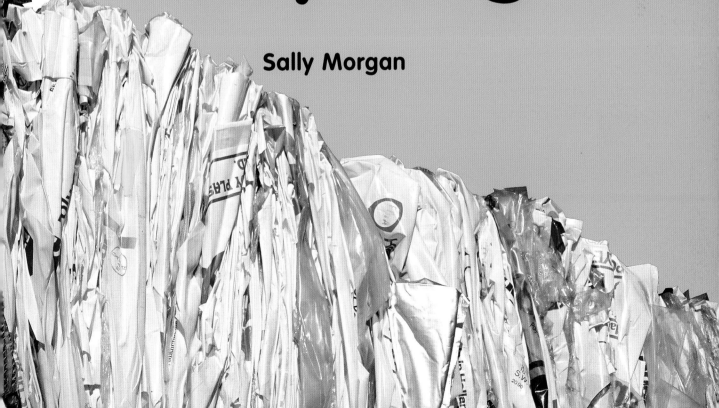

Cherrytree Books are distributed in the United States
by Black Rabbit Books, P.O. Box 3263, Mankato, MN 56002

Printed in China.

Library of Congress Cataloging-in-Publication Data

Morgan, Sally.
  Waste and recycling / Sally Morgan.
    p. cm. -- (Helping our planet)
  Includes index.
  ISBN 978-1-84234-608-2 (lib. bd.)
  1. Refuse and refuse disposal--Juvenile literature. 2. Recycling (Waste, etc.)--Juvenile literature.
I. Title. II. Series.

TD792.M663 2011
363.72'8--dc22

2010000037

First Edition
9 8 7 6 5 4 3 2 1

First published in 2009 by Evans Brothers Ltd.
2A Portman Mansions, Chiltern Street, London W1U 6NR, United Kingdom

Copyright © Evans Brothers Ltd. 2009

Picture Credits:
Cover: (main) Ray Roberts, inset, left to right: Luc Hosten, Lorenzo Lees, Vicki Coombs; title page Alex
Bartel; p6 Vicki Coombs; p7 Linda Whatmore; pp8 & 9 Wayne Lawler; p10 Luc Hosten; p11 left Erik
Schaffer right Katy Peters; p12 Ray Roberts; p13 Chinch Gryniewicz; p14 Mark Tweedie; p15 Alan
Towse; p16 Neil and Ruth Thomson; p17 Kate Peters; p18 Edward Bent; p19 Ceanne Jansen; pp20 and
21 Ray Roberts; p22 Kevin King; p23 Alan Towse; p24 Vicki Coombs; p25 Ed Maynard; p26 Angela
Hampton; p27 Tony Page

Printed on chlorine free paper from sustainably managed sources.

Contents

Everyday Waste

Every day we throw things away — plastic bags and bottles, old newspapers, broken toys, or unwanted clothes. Industry, schools, hospitals, and farms create waste too. People have to find ways of dealing with the mountains of waste that we all produce.

▼ How much trash does your family produce each week?

People living in the more developed countries, such as the United States, Australia, and Britain, produce much more waste than people living in the less developed parts of the world, such as Botswana or Tanzania. In these less developed countries, people try to put unwanted things to a new use.

People have made the walls of this thatched hut in Botswana from old aluminum cans.

What Can Be Done?

We can reduce the amount of trash that we throw away by keeping back anything that can be reused or recycled. We can recycle glass, metal, plastic, paper, cardboard, old clothes, and used batteries.

Taking Waste Away

Most household waste is collected and taken to a landfill. A landfill is a huge hole in the ground that is slowly filled with waste. Once the hole is full, people spread soil on top. Then the land can be used as a park or for farming.

You choose

Is it a good idea to bury waste? Would you like to live near to a landfill site? What else could we do with trash?

Trash is dumped onto a landfill.

In some places, people take waste to a local dump and burn it there. Sometimes they use a specially built incinerator to burn waste. We can use the heat from burning waste to make electricity. However, the best way to tackle the waste problem is to recycle as much as we can.

The waste in this dump is burned rather than buried.

Reduce, Reuse, and Recycle

There are three important words linked to reducing waste — reduce, reuse, and recycle.

To reduce is to create less waste by not buying something in the first place. To reuse something means to use it again or put it to a new use. For example, sometimes we can mend old clothes rather than throwing them away.

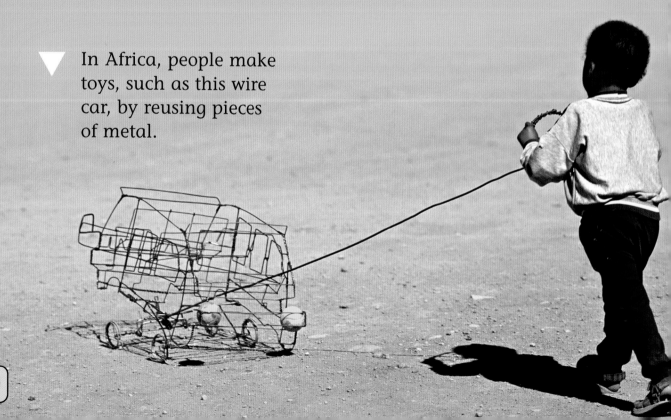

▼ In Africa, people make toys, such as this wire car, by reusing pieces of metal.

To recycle means to take waste and turn it into something new — for example, making used metal cans into new cans.

People have made these handbags from recycled car tires and potato chip bags.

People will reuse these tires to form the bottom layer of a new road.

Find Out More

Learn more about the 3Rs — reduce, reuse, recycle — by visiting this website http://www.kidsrecyclingzone.com/.

Saving Paper

We use paper for writing on, for printing books and newspapers, for packaging, advertising, and much more. Most paper is made from fast-growing trees, such as pine and eucalyptus. People cut down trees and mash up the wood into a pulp, which is made into paper.

▼ These children are making sheets of writing paper from recycled paper.

We can recycle paper. People collect old newspaper and cardboard and add them to the pulp mix. This saves energy and reduces the number of trees that are chopped down.

What Can Be Done?

Paper can be made from other plants too, such as bamboo, papyrus, reeds, jute, and cotton. These plants are important in less developed countries where wood is in short supply.

We can use shredded paper to insulate the walls of new homes.

Recycling Metal

Metals, such as iron, copper, aluminum, and gold, are useful materials. People use them to make a variety of things, from jewelry to machinery. Metals are found in rocks. Removing the metal from the rocks creates a lot of waste. It is damaging to the environment, too. It's important to recycle as much metal as we can.

People heat aluminum until it melts and pour it into molds. The aluminum cools and forms solid blocks. Then the blocks can be melted and the aluminum used again.

We can recycle metal over and over again. We can heat old metal objects until they melt and make them into new objects. The more metals are recycled, the less rock is dug from the ground. Recycling metal saves energy and transport too.

At this recycling center people make sure all the metal cans are separated from the other trash before they recycle them.

You Choose

What sort of drink container do you think is better for the environment — a plastic bottle or an aluminum can?

What Happens to Glass?

Glass is another very useful material. We use it to make windows, for example, and containers such as bottles and jars. People make glass by heating sand and limestone together until they melt and become a liquid. The hot liquid can then be turned into different shapes.

▼ We can reuse some glass objects. Can you see how someone has reused the glass in this pill bottle to make a spice jar?

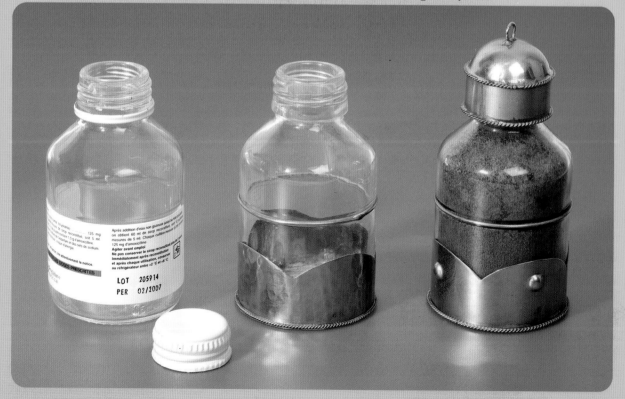

As well as using glass objects again, we can recycle them. Recycling glass is easy. The old glass is crushed and heated until it melts. Recycling old glass saves energy as well as the raw materials needed for new glass.

These children have taken glass bottles to a bottle bank for recycling.

Find Out More

More glass is recycled than any other material. Recycled glass can be made into new bottles, into jewelry, or even crushed to make garden paths. Find out more at http://www.olliesworld.com/.

Plastic Problems

Plastic waste causes lots of problems because it takes many years to break down. This means it stays in the environment where it gets blown around and becomes entangled in trees and fences. Often plastic bags end up in oceans where they harm animals.

▼ People have thrown away plastic, which has washed up on this beach in Wales.

You Choose

Do you think it is a good idea to stop people using plastic bags?

We can recycle plastic. People can make many new things from recycled plastic, including garden furniture, fencing, pots, and even clothes.

It makes sense to recycle plastic. Plastic is made from oil and our supply of oil is running out. Recycling saves valuable oil, and reduces litter too.

We can break up plastic into tiny pieces and melt them in a factory. Then we can make the melted plastic into new objects.

Recycling Cars and Electrical Goods

Sometimes people buy new computers, cell phones, and televisions just because they want the latest designs. There is often nothing wrong with the old ones they are replacing. The more new machines people buy, the more materials are needed to make them.

However, people can give in their old machines for recycling. Then the materials can be used to make new machines.

This sculpture is made from old bits of electrical and electronic equipment.

We can recycle old cars. People can remove the useful parts and sell them to people who need to repair their own cars. We can recycle the metal and plastic from cars too. Even old tires have lots of new uses. Look back at the pictures on page 11.

What Can Be Done?

We can break up old fridges and recycle the materials they are made from.

Food Waste

Shopping at a supermarket is easy, but people often buy more food than they need. About one third of all the food we buy ends up thrown away. This is a huge waste of resources.

Farmers use energy when they plow their fields and harvest their crops. Farm animals produce waste too.

Then people create more waste in the factories when they process and package the food. We also use fuel in the trucks that deliver the food to the stores.

 We can put leftover fruit and vegetables on a compost pile. Later in the year, the compost is ready to put on the garden to help plants grow.

If we reduce food waste, we can help to save energy and resources. More importantly, we will be using fewer food crops. This means there will be more for people who need them in other parts of the world.

▼ Worms help to turn scrap fruit and vegetables into compost. They are nature's recyclers.

Find Out More

Find out how you could set up a composting project in your garden or school. Go to http://www.epa.gov/epawaste/conserve/rrr/composting/basic.htm.

Recycling Clothes

We make clothes from natural materials such as cotton and wool, and artificial fibers such as nylon and polyester.

People spray crops such as cotton with chemicals to kill pests and disease. These chemicals harm the environment. Nylon and polyester come from oil. So if we reduce the number of clothes we buy, we can reduce the damage we do to the environment.

▼ The cotton in the clothes we wear starts off as plants like these.

▲ These people are sorting old clothes, picking out items that can be worn again. They will sell the clothes in stores to raise money for charity.

What Can Be Done?

We can recycle old clothes, sheets, towels, and even shoes. People can use the material from old clothes and make it into new clothes. We can cut up old underwear and T-shirts and use them as cleaning cloths. We can shred old clothes into little pieces as stuffing for cushions and mattresses.

Reducing Your Waste

If everybody reduced their waste and recycled as much as possible, resources and energy would be saved and there would be less waste harming the environment.

There are lots of simple ways to reduce waste. Avoid buying goods that have lots of packaging so there is less to throw away.

When you go shopping take a reusable bag rather than using a new plastic bag on each trip.

Reuse and recycle whatever you can. You and your friends can save paper by writing on both sides of every sheet. You can save plastic by choosing reusable water bottles and lunchboxes. If you have a compost pile, you can add shredded paper and cardboard to it, as well as vegetable waste. There are lots of things you can do to make a difference.

We can recycle batteries of all different shapes and sizes. People can reuse the useful materials.

Find Out More

See if you can help to reduce the amount of waste produced at your school. Find out more at: http://www.guvswd.org/ed.

Glossary

artificial made by people

compost pile a heap of rotting materials such as fruit and vegetable waste that becomes something we can use to help plants grow well

environment the natural world that surrounds us. Water, air, plants, and animals are all part of the natural environment

incinerator a structure in which people burn waste at high temperatures

insulate to fill with a material that stops heat escaping and so keeps us warm

landfill a large hole in the ground where waste is buried

less developed country a country that is not wealthy, such as Ethiopia or Sudan

more developed country a wealthy country such as the United States or Canada

plow to turn over soil so that it is ready for planting crops

polyester a fiber that is made from oil; it is often used to make clothes

pulp paper or wood that people have broken up into a mash

raw materials materials such as aluminum that we use to make into something new, such as storage cans for food and drink

recycle to use unwanted materials to make something new

reduce to lessen, produce less

reuse to use again

shredded torn into tiny pieces

Index

Numbers in **bold** refer to pictures.